ABOUT THE AUTHOR

Caitlin Stobie was born in South Africa and holds a PhD from the University of Leeds. She is a winner of the Douglas Livingstone Creative Writing Competition and the Heather Drummond Memorial Prize for Poetry, and was named by South African literary journal *New Contrast* as one of the country's 'rising stars' in poetry. Her first monograph, *Abortion Ecologies in Southern African Fiction*, is forthcoming with Bloomsbury Academic. She is a Lecturer in Creative Writing at the University of Leeds.

'Startlingly vivid, tender, and surprising, once I began *Thin Slices* I couldn't stop. Caitlin Stobie has written a collection that is at once far-ranging and intimate in both its subject matter and voice. Ecological and bodily in its energy, this book carries us from South Africa to Leeds via oceans and swimming pools and the magnetized view of a membrane. Stobie expertly cuts through public and private spaces and sits us amongst women in hospital waiting rooms and with lovers in a new embrace. Drenched in colour and full of texture and smell, these are poems to be relished and savoured again and again. And yet within this richness *Thin Slices* takes on difficult and deeply personal subject matter and handles it with sensitivity and grace. Stobie offers an unflinching and precise gaze on everything she examines. Each poem invites us to look and feel on a microscopic level, and to find beauty and revelation in the thin slices of the world that are laid out before us. I love every bit of this remarkable collection.'
– *Hannah Copley*

'These poems glow like a nighttime bridge in a great city-port, or like the imagining of a Dutch master painter, or like the bioluminescence of life-forms known dearly by scientists. They are beautifully intelligent, and seem to grow into being as they are read. Stobie's lyrical and visual craftsmanship gives these poems strong force, gently applied. A child's trip to the aquarium, a lover's memory spanning oceans, the troublesome and glorious business of leaky bodies: in each scene and situation, the poet tendrils and tunnels a kind, startling way.'
– *Anthony Vahni Capildeo*

Caitlin Stobie
Thin Slices

VERVE
POETRY PRESS

PUBLISHED BY VERVE POETRY PRESS
https://vervepoetrypress.com
mail@vervepoetrypress.com

FIRST PUBLISHED NOV 2022

Printed and bound in the UK
by ImprintDigital, Exeter

ISBN: 978-1-913917-20-3

Cover image by Zexi Xu

to Q. Mapukata, for reading

and to the Oxford Non-book Club, for not

CONTENTS

Waking a Sleeping Rabbit by Surrounding Him
with Grapes   12

Carried   13

Gastronomer   14

Binge Museum   16

Gardener   18

Skeleton Equation   19

Awakening   20

A Fig   21

Five Ways of Looking at a Period   23

Echo's Reflection   25

Eve   28

I worry of   30

—

Bilayer   32

The Bridge   33

Video Games   35

Birth Control Blues   36

Exams   37

The Hit   38

War Paint   39

Striking Rocks   41

Ngiyakuthanda   42

Offerings to a God   43

Jealousy Experiment   45

Frozen in time and space   50

—

W   52

Potential   56

Gentled   57

Monarch   59

Christmas Quartet   60

The Game   64

Ballad of a Good Boy   66

Even Birds   67

Whale's Love Song   69

Bees never flew to me   70

Hum   71

The Little Things   72

Swimming Lessons   73

Acknowledgements and Notes

Thin Slices

In microbiology, ultramicrotomy is a method of cutting specimens into thin slices (0.1 mcm or less) with a fine glass or diamond knife for examination under an electron microscope.

'Thin-slicing is not an exotic gift. It is a central part of what it means to be human. We thin-slice whenever we meet a new person or have to make sense of something quickly or encounter a novel situation. We thin-slice because we have to, and we come to rely on that ability because there are lots of hidden fists out there, lots of situations where careful attention to the details of a very thin slice, even for no more than a second or two, can tell us an awful lot.'

— Malcolm Gladwell, *Blink: The Power of Thinking Without Thinking*

'If the end of one's youth is a thin slice of cheese I ate mine standing in that room. I was there because I was hungry. That's all.'

— Eileen Myles, *Chelsea Girls*

Waking a Sleeping Rabbit by Surrounding Him with Grapes

In this frame, I am the fruits of tight skin
lined artfully round your twitching

The still in still life
as buck legs stretch
to pulse and jump in dreams

You honk and squeak through
imagined banana bites,
parsley roots and dillweed
(you've yet to smell red dripping sweet)

As an eyelid peels its lens
we are frozen in symbiosis –
you, lying side-like, looking shot,
me, a membrane, doubled womb –
and it's unclear who's the sacrifice

God is the hand that splits me even
now, as your teeth range free from
sleeping to waking, free for so long from
decaying till time coils and I am once more a vine, vining

Round a rabbit-shaped negative space
waiting for the thumbnail's knife
to slice me open, please

Carried

Little legs
lithe and wide as bicycle tyres
are wrapped around a mother's torso.

The woman is silent, working.
Her koala-child in red-blanket-attachment
stares. The look says,

The continent will carry me
when I'm no longer on her back.

If I ever have a daughter
I will travel with her
tied to my spine and say,

My land taught me this:
love doesn't stop
when you let go

or leave.

Gastronomer

When some remember their elders
they taste sugar and cream.
Gran, I can't recall
a single dish you made,

but I still smell
the citrus you
rubbed between rocks
and dangled on my knees.

That December
(heaving with cicadas)
I lost milk teeth
on White Rabbits:

a sweet for each
seamless
dive.

You trained me
to play Chopsticks, poorly,
and rolled cold marbles
in Chinese checkers.

At night you taught me rummy.

I did not say
damn, and never
bent from the waist.
Returning

from our Burmese neighbours'
you made me
scrub my hands.

Now, remembered lemons
in untrimmed grass
look the same
as the dregs in this glass.
The past is no gold filter,
just a moral of bad taste.

How do I repress
the expectations
you birthed in me?

Binge Museum

all daughters are born sleek
with a map between their gums

& all mothers glean recipes
from their grandmothers' gardens

by the time they can read
most daughters are already visitors
of the binge museum

they cut glass eyes
on curated levels
of bacon flavouring
& MSG

a congenital weakness
for galleries of yeast & bone
halls of corn & salt
but not fat – no, never that

it's more a craving for love, looted
artefact that had never been
theirs to receive, the mothers
who choke down husks
of love, love only

to spit them up again

the statues who cannot see
how their grandmothers & others'

are children inside, hungry
to be taken home

Gardener

Dandelions' motes in the air,
the dewy fade in your hair,
a few stars pushing out:
all insubstantial glitter.
Your vowels formed a young orchard.

That night you bared a scar,
a pit I dared not lip.
The next I dreamed of creeping
fingers – precious rooting.
With small mourning, to spring I woke.

The heart wants.
The heart wants.
Oh, how the heart plants
in wrong places: wild
clover too late to sow.

Skeleton Equation

Lying on the cured veld
we must have looked
like a skeleton equation

I couldn't tell where
my lines ended
and your bones began

It was just a flurry
of fingers, legs
and imbalanced lips:
too many of them
yet only two of us
crunching dead grass

Our jigsaw thoughts were missing
molecules: all yang and not
a spot of yin

Less was the matter
when you kissed me upside-down;
that way you thought
I was smiling too

Awakening

in the tenth month   it began.

the night   the moon pulled
you came in   my dreams,
crushed   and cut
red velvet   against my lips.

we rutted without a kiss.

unrefined, we were   freed of sensibility:
fermenting   bad timing,
cocoa and vanilla   and a muted roux
that sours   in beetroot mix.

I woke to   a bewitching bleed,
a softness   unknown, yet
you'd tasted like   an old favourite.

A Fig

Forbidden starts with a fig tree.
This is how the Bible begins
and also my belief
though mine stems
not from the leaves, but eating.
Uterine pulp,
endometrial seeds:
these are made in part
from the bodies of pollinators,
wingless wasps. (Thank Aristotle
for this naked knowledge.)
Some thirsts are forever
trapped beneath skin –
fresh air, sleep,
the mortal caterwauling of curiosity –
but hunger
dies with an insect
digested through plant flesh.
(It's easy not to eat
like a lady
with this deathsmilk in mind.)
Other roots of disgust
include: flushing through
a first menses, feeling heavy
and cystic and thick, and
Pentecostal sex education.
(If only the milk of human
kindness alone

could feed a body that bruises
for being, for seeing, for knowing
too much.)
O fruit-that-consumes,
slimy ouroboros:
the rats eat you
for they cannot read.
I push away plates
and like to think I'm wiser.

Five Ways of Looking at a Period

I
A ruined pool party.
Cat-scratch in the pants.
Thighs tight and plastic-wrapped.
Luxury cotton towel sex.
Soggy apologies like *I'm-on-my*.

II
Peach's pit-flesh.
Cherryburst anemone.
Pomegranate plasma.
Beet-cloaked clover.
Hibiscus nimbus.

III
Brings muddy sleep, long as gumtrees.
Quenches anxiety with slippy lip sap.
Approves full-bellied foods, potatoes, ginger root.
Pulls distraction's tubers and unearths certainty.
Teaches how to stand being lonely.

IV
When eggs crack jokes about coming first.
When proteins drag blush over queenly cheeks.
When lipids birth another month's dead doulas.
When sickle cells group under coven moons.
Hello, capillaries. Hello again, iron age friends.

V

Cramping coloured like conception's twinge.
Craving the ever-ready chocolate advent.
Carving papayas with turmeric fingers.
Wishing for its mercurochrome tinge.
Then, sudden puddle of *thank-fuck*.

Echo's Reflection

I

When Narcissus asked Echo's reflection to bear his child, her face fell open in two ways. He froze. He boiled over her prognosis. Some say she should have sensed bitter waters – yes & no. At 19, she didn't know daffodils choke romance from the rose.

II

in love & pregnancy: fell, fell
both verbs stressed as if ill as

in coming down with him. in the early
days i had no reason 2 seek thru reeds

4 bloodwort & juniper leaves but the possibilities
repeated in dreams: ossified creatures in the belly

III

He hunted Echo's body for discourse on tragedy. The academic daddies & catamites cried what a scholar! such theories! For Narcissus predicted the rise of Oedipus. He'd show them, he insisted, in his thesis. They'd see.

IV

as selected host of these pathogens & genes, my voice
auditioned 4 victim roles: this i had 2 learn 2 admit

V

Each clean day was a week. Months were centuries. In her 21st year,
when the herbs didn't work, she found a novel where someone got lost
on the way to an abortionist: the woman neither cried nor died &
she stopped at a shopfront post-operation to admire crystallised figs
& pears that shimmered like insects, like possibilities. She bought every
dried fruit, gorging on life & choice with no debate in sight & truth fell
from the fiction like petals.

VI

no & no & – so
she spoke. Narcissus started
skipping his own lectures & concerned
members of the academy asked Echo where he was, as
if she had graduated to mother, no longer mere understudy
but she was done with Jocasta's lines. Sometimes he'd lie outside
her home or leave 20 messages in a row about embryos but she floated
in a feverdream of Alone. She found taffeta curtains & bathed by their
teal light, staring at curlicues of air bricks that looked like clear
wombs, fallopian tubes. Her old supervisor & his wife (two
metaphysicians who grew seedlings) said she started to
glow, to bloom. So she rose by writing
a treatise on agency & so on
& on & on & –

VII

lightyears later, living in the lee, I received a
throwaway message with familiar grammar:

I'll show u, u'll see. *dear parasite of the past*
ur myths r revisionist; no Iynx bird was borne

by me. I chose 4 my abandoned inner
children & the opposite of tragedy. 4

gone as the foetus is, there always was &
will b shadows of u, narcissus, within me.

in time I will meet a shepherd & carry a lamb
named Iambe. it's enough 4 now 2 give thanks

4 what u never meant 2 teach
4 the inner mirrors & beasts

Eve

Through the screen's gloam
in two dimensions, yes, you're there:
our anonymous babe. My entire
life seeds in your swimming digits.

Not two days later, something
blooms where I wake.
Limbless sea-woman, I refuse to rise, to make
the loss complete till he finds me.

For days I sketch the Birth
of Venus from the couch.
For weeks I teethe green fruit
and finger the dictionary till the

eve he catches me
test-trying dictions
we no longer need. He does not ask.
But diving

into my cunning he runs
his mouth, tipping a litany:
each syllable, our hurt.
Every name is an irony.

Later we unfurl and
cede to sleep. In time
I shuck off the covers,
donate the books and booties, taste

life's thorny oysters.
And yet some evenings still
I ask Eden how once
was enough to make you.

I worry of

everything. Perhaps an ectopic
growth: lying prone inside five months.
Register likely signed in absentia.

The midwife, possibly a ghost
(only there when eyes are closed).
In the theatre wake-dream doctors discuss rugby, maybe.

And what if the scream is breech – flesh hot as if tearing
apart? Conceivably neither he nor she and the surgeons will not see
which sex is less cursed.

Worst risk of all: to birth a perfect girl
(velvet-naped, luckybean)
and feel, completely, nothing.

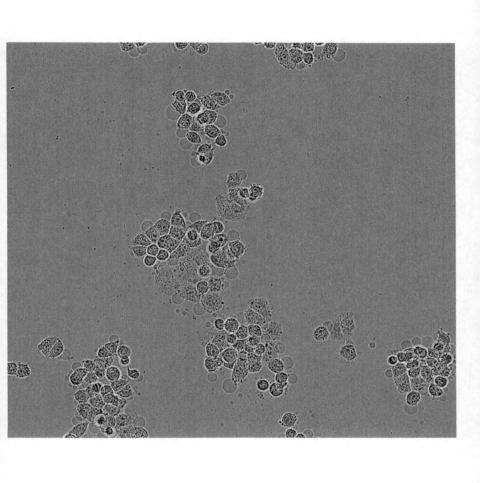

Bilayer

a
being living
yet a beast borne
neither by woman nor man a
lone made thing
matters what
is this
design
in the
walls all
cell   parts
look   like
some   awe
twists   of
fate   and
signs   co-
in   -cide

-cide   in
co-   signs
and   fate
of   twists
awe   some
like   look
parts   cell
all   walls
the in
design
this is
what matters
thing made lone
a man nor woman by neither
borne beast a yet
living being
a

The Bridge

There's a bridge near a town I lived
and no water flows below it.
After two decades of peace,
new human rights and rallies,
the dam's toxins still
leak unequally.

There are stock photographs of boys
from that township and others.
All sip taps with bent hands,
seemingly genuflecting to something
out of frame.
Zoom over 8000 miles north and

there's The Bridge Inn in Kirkstall
where a rough year's floods
drove two men to drink in the burst riverbank.
Sat waist-deep. The manager's words were,
I stood and shouted at the water,
but it didn't seem to do much.

There is a way to read this pixelated image
for what it isn't and what it impacts:
pints and water, rising tides and drought,
the Northern Powerhouse and universal South
bridge generations
until, rising from all depths of contradiction,

there's an inkling
those boys across the globe aren't kneeling
to the gracious saviours we'd think.
Maybe they too just grew sick
of standing, of shouting
when all they wanted was a drink.

Video Games

Up late at night wrapped in telephone wires – remember what
        desire seemed like?;
Up close in a screen of black we met, that first real-life night,
        sneaking out &
Down by the dam; in a friend's two-man tent our four hands
        turned one &
Down was the little bend I showed you how to press (deep in the
        boy inside me)

Left to figure girls alone with no cheat codes, I liked how you
        never said princess;
Right or not, even the mean things were left unsaved, erased; like
        that evening a
Left turn led to flat tyres & for three hours in your dad's car we
        lay unmapped together
Right beneath stars, legs wrapped like broken VCRs (all lips &
        fingers willingly lost)

Be it legal or wrong, we played consent by taking turns, being
        genderless & free;
A decade later no man matches that game concentration; in my
        movie-memory still you
Start clamping close, close, thighs closed, & don't stop (least not
        till I ask)

Birth Control Blues

Every time I take
The pill, I feel closer to
The day I'll expire

At least they don't say
'Mother Time'; that too would be
A bad reminder

Exams

Plenty girls worry now, the doctor says,
eyes fast on the shock
of a belly stretched at fifty years.
Women, that is,

and up snaps the speculum.
She tells of one patient –
an exchange student – who didn't bleed for ten months:
anxious about exams.

The girl thought it was a curse! she brays.
Imagine. I do not want to
because the men who made this tool
practised on undrugged slaves.

Anyway, it'll work out okay for you eh?
Just tell the old man to get the snip.
If he wants, that is. Plenty people
having kids like this, not too many risks.

A wife with braids is in the hallway.
From her size, her eyes, it is also too late.
Behind another door someone soothes
ooh, yes, that's a good girl.

The Hit

I once knew a dentist
who judged others by
their bitemarks.

Next I met an optician.
What she saw in people
was the colours of their eyes.

Then I met a cardiologist
who stared at strangers' fists.
I asked for my heart's size.

'I'm not sure, kid,' he replied.
'All I know's how to hit
when a hidden fist arrives.'

War Paint

Performing our pain.
At war with ourselves.
In this pageant

visors of mascara,
grenades of painted nails
are what we've got to fight with.

Our lips
are crimson minesweepers – yet
light, like a pair of phantom limbs.

Our breasts,
the inspiration
of songs and sonnets,

become tin mugs
from which future regiments
drink.

Our wombs
(those zero-gravity airlocks)
tick slightly too slowly:

the offbeat march
of the last
soldiers in a line.

Only the scruffs of our necks
and the spaces between
our shoulder-blades are no man's

land. A trench
between head
and heart.

Striking Rocks

Olive Schreiner is buried with Samuel Cronwright-Schreiner, their one-day-old baby, and her dog Nita on Buffelskop mountain in South Africa

'Wathint' abafazi,
wathint' imbokodo,
uza kufa!
When you strike the women,
you strike a rock,
you will be crushed!'

– Freedom song from the 1956 Women's March against apartheid pass laws

Ingrid and Virginia were taken with
the waves, but you, Olive, dreamed of being
exhumed in the foggy Camdeboo. Some
mark the sky when ascending – harking black
eagles over sarcophagus – but the
truth is you loved that solid, stolid earth.
Husband, dog, human bundle: all took ten
men to move, yet your will was mineral.
The locusts of '86 led preachers
to curse the mountain for its thunder storms,
the eternal aversion of flora.
With buffaloes they died; the peak persists.
Olive, you embraced women as rocks; still
the words are live, triggering lightning strikes

Ngiyakuthanda

In Zulu
there is no difference
between like
and love.

Between 'I want to hold your hand'
and 'Can I see your ring finger?'
Between wanting to know where you stand
and wanting a one-night stand.

Between the sheets,
between two lives,
just one phrase makes it
come together.

I'm still not sure
whether open interpretation
makes love
easier, or just

lost in translation.

Offerings to a God

C. asks if you know how
to spot the heart of a poet.
Says if you cut it open
you'll find
yellowing handwriting
stuck to the ventricles.
If you put it
under a microscope
you'll see music sheets
covering the veins:
a larghissimo tempo
written for a broken drum.
Squeeze it
and blood
the colour of a minor chord
will stain your hands.
But the easiest way to tell
C. preaches, is by noting
the heart is neither whole
nor halved.
There are Roman numerals
scratched onto scar tissue,
craters and holes dividing
lines by zero–

O yes, C., it's true
but the flock sees more
than you believe we do.
Each line you think to write
about somebody new
is really all for you:
offerings to a god
who doesn't believe in themselves.

Jealousy Experiment

Colour Question

Green is not the colour of love.
Some might see this as cheating –
to frame an opener in negative terms –
but isn't that how we approach all tones?

It's not pink, more purple. So it goes.
No, green will never be
the colour of love. That title is thought
to belong to its antithesis, red, right
at the other end of the spectrum –
even then, popular belief is wrong.

Blue is really where that feeling belongs.
Solnit knew this; Nelson, too.
Mitchell sang it and Maroh even drew it:
the warmest colour. A colour for two.

I am all out of questions about love
but can green ever be
without a little blue?

Likely Hypothesis

I send green hearts to platonic friends. I hide them beneath others' likes and effusive comments. This is safe love: when they don't respond, I know not to grieve. When they post a picture with someone new, I never feel envy.

Many languages use the same words for both blue and green. In Xhosa and Zulu, -*luhlaza* is used semi-contextually: people add *like the sky* or *like grass*, even when speaking of technology.

I think about aquamarine and cyan and liking you more than I should do. I wonder how to transmute affection: a thumbs-up minus the likeness of blue.

If I could, I would fool us both with a lime heart and mean it, too. I would reverse our alchemy – green lions spewing out the sun – and stop writing *I* and *you*.

If the second person is blue, then the first is verdant.

Green Test

the year I didn't know you were partnered
cracked an age of iron with silicon light
the geology of our conversations
open like sliced ammonites

well

                well well?

what's appening

                what a well-wishing

asking if you're doing well!

                you know...

in your bones?

                so humerus

Slick as moss, we omitted *I* from sentences and email threads. We
believed subjectless verbs could still the depths of intimacy. Yet, with
each pastel message, something greener was growing – a puff of algae
fed by water that's diseased.

Denial Analysis

the aged question is
not about eggs and hens
or men and women being friends
but gender-neutral green

is transmogrified into some such inquiry
at the hands of curious parties
like the painters who can never leave
Eve or Adam without a leaf

we imagined a better question would be
what does natural even mean
as sediment settled deep in our molar teeth
cavities from *sent*, the mints of feeling seen

who else received the gleam
of your inorganic sentiments
what is lust but pyrite
in the canary cry of day

yet for all my magma
within the fearful heart of

some faultlines surely lie
she who didn't ask

sloppy as yolk
when archiving denial

the corollary follows
you see your own yellow

Fossil Conclusion

Closer than the heavens or sea, mundane as a membrane, inside you
and me – between all friends there's the ghost of green.

As the coastline compounds sea
creatures and petrified leaves, we lie
limestone, a record no stylus can repeat.

No more blue pixels, the ticks stay grey, *delivered*
but never seen. That's the problem with fossils:
for the longest time
we played believe with what they mean.

Frozen in time and space

but also just on the grid:
this black ice attracted
to copper, to thickening,
to messing everything up.
We're in the control room; down
behind the glass is a microscope
double a human's height.
What we can see: metal, a vat of
nitrogen, university branding.
What's visible thanks to the screen,
what's human-made yet mimicking
the near-atomic parts of me
is a membrane within a membrane
next to some dozens of the same
and that's just the one frame.
There are hundreds on each grid;
'I'm looking at 8 lacy grids today'.
Small wonder then
when we catch a vesicle
at the rare second of bursting,
ruptured membrane still
a blobby line of light – or
is it my astigmatised eye?
You decide:

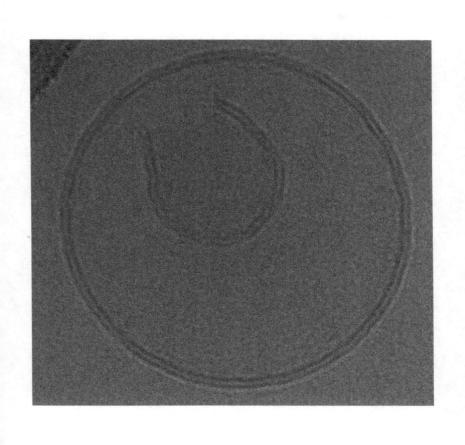

W

After Tony Harrison

Last May I cycled to the cemetery
to see old graffiti, the Vs, your task.
All I found was dog shit and dried lilies,
then drifting litter: a surgical mask.

Who am I to write this reply?
Thin slices of an accent, southerner
by way of Africa: best believe I,
too, hate grave advice from foreigners.

But someone has to start with the questions.
Again I try, fail, trying to go on.
Each year brings more floods and man-made seasons;
what if we united, but did it wrong?

Walking long ago, counting cracks, I asked
Why's the street wet? to a boy from a band.
He pointed his free hand. A drunk's turned back.
If you were a man, love, you'd understand.

On Saturdays all men came out alleys
to grope the slippery centre of Leeds.
The city's never been so lively
we chanted, dodging vomit every week.

Tony, you know what's meant when I say 'all'
and 'men'. For in the Brude and Chunk you'd see
– even in Wharf's safest toilet stall –
them slits slashed clean between two widened Vs.

In '85 it was swear words lads sprayed
round town. Now 'cunt' is on discount, reduced.
'The versuses of life', 'man and wife': splayed
like legs in the cubicle W.

They say in Shakespeare's day, 'cunt' was 'nothing'.
Lately, the male organ's tune is the same.
Why else, when we protest, would some men sing
Not all? Their chorus is not to complain.

Worse still are the racists, the EDL
with their own slogans of 'nothing' and 'not'.
All lives matter, they say, but they fear hell
is other people talking, taking their lot.

In the year of the rat, trafficked pangolins and bats,
lines between species were ever troubling
and as humans destroyed their habitats
the Vs and our visions were doubling.

It should not have taken a pandemic
to see that we need to set this right.
Yet between the blurring Vs came an epic
chorus chiming *Not all!* and *Mine! Mine! Mine!*

When you can't walk at night without keys between your fists,
what do you rhyme that with?
Where can you wander without watchmen if you're Black?
(The chorus warbles: *Not all! Mine! Mine! Mine!*)

We bicker and consumerist excess continues, the Vs are
Ws, too many to write –
when that man said *You wouldn't understand,*
why did I not drop his hand?

Last May, I traced letters on graves. Cee, u, en, tee.
Much ado about the bard, in your poem, Tony,
but Shakespeare leads to one more query:
if 'nothing' is sacred, then what does that make me?

Laughter bloomed. *You – you stupid animals,*
cats-ears nodded as if to say,
you're nowt special. Blood, meat, bones, minerals:
all beasts turn to feed when they decay.

Then it hit me: the double-u in nowt.
Same as millennials' scrawl in toilets,
but the slashed command signified now
both\holy/everything\and/jack-shit.

Like headstones leaning together, four lines
in a consonant, a cuss, or a poem
may remind us of the beasts inside –
or so I liked to hum as I headed home.

So home I ride – for some of us never
felt safe outside, for I am no bride, no double you
see (in my head the man says, 'n
anyway, love, how's about you make tea).

No. Home to a room and view of my own,
to the place where I grandmother myself.
I doze in a rented room, alone,
old words of new worlds lining my bookshelf.

Reader, how will Leeds look next year?
When do death-tolls become a wake-up call?
When we rebuild, will we remember nowt?
Will nothing have changed at all?

Potential

those were the days
of rusted jungle gyms
and crinkled toes

the days
when our clothes smelled
of Being Afraid of the Deep End

when taken to aquariums, we wondered
if the adults knew we were just a shoal
being watched by fish

we wrote letters on mulberry leaves
in words that didn't exist
or weren't meant to

our purple-stained tongues
(so strong, so young)
had the potential to learn Latin

we smelled sour-rain baking jasmine roads;
the secret ingredient
to feeling close to home

we were never in too deep
possessed by flight dreams in our sleep
we could have been anything

Gentled

After Douglas Livingstone

Eleven years after you first
graced our lawn with drawn-out yowls
and yellowed claws,
we have to make the stilted trip.

A receptionist asks for your name.
Is it still the same?
The check-up senses
you were never gentled

but today you are lime-eyed and tame.
My little lost one,
my myth of bone,
stripes of the tiger in zebra chrome.

What an unusual coat,
the woman across says.
Her dark kitten stares.
I smile despite the diagrams of fleas
warnings of disease
and boxes of organic dog biscuits.

A parrot carols its curtain call and
we are next to be shepherded in.
Claws discording metal, crawling the
table,
you are

pewter-framed. Mute.
Hot as a crushed bud.

There's no defining
final moment, no
shaking out a last lungful,
just the hum of fluorescent tubes.

It's okay. Take two tissues.
I stay until your saliva dries.
On my way outside
with an uncanny cage
the black cat wails; her human
turns away.

Monarch

Black-veined orange,
the Latin proves it:
yours is a regal species.

But now you're dead
centre in an unmoving wiper
(I, driver, was too late to swerve).

At speed, your wings still
serve their purpose –
fluttering hurricanes somewhere.

Christmas Quartet

Eve

Militant as in vegan
or as in gammon jowls?
Someone had to ask
(the ham couldn't).

Cutting rind of swine in
pushed-around peas
for disinterested index fingers,
trying not to touch grease.

Did you watch some cartoons today.
Which one is your favourite. Oh you
like Peppa. Your auntie also cares for pigs.
Pity you can't teach her how to eat!

Day

Velvet dress on niece fits loosely:
maybe better that way, but next year
may be too small. Every try a failure; ever failing,
trying again to resist spiced biscuits.
Fintan craves taste of Space
Ice Cream sourced online
(no cows harmed)*.
Baby plays with gift wrapping; later
found chewing ethical festive cards.
Ah well, thought counts, *no carbs in that*
but definitely dairy
so no thanks, no matter

Dinner

potato, potato, gravy, non-buttered potato.
beans, carrot, littlebitmore potato – goosefat
maybe? spit!
no cauliflower (cheese)
but butternut squash is yes.
must make like this.

smell a song of pudding the way mother used to
cake iced snowmen up the plate.
best bone china all alight.
jesus is brandy cruelty-free

Boxing

*

~~no~~
returns and
amazon thanks you
for forests of collapsed cardboard
raining out back doors. plasticine and paper
film shame
with sharpies scratching labels,
unread name and address by sender ~~in~~visibly there
saying *what if Stephen sees*
the dead trees and turkeys, the whey and the
lactose in the biscuits and cauli-cheese and the margarine
used to ~~de~~-butter those potatoes.
tearing packages can ~~neither~~ undo email receipts ~~nor~~ the deals we
s t r e t c h :
~~non~~-bio
degradable bag
leaves coal-dust hands

The Game

the packaging
said 100% natural
genuine material
organic ingredients
locally produced

the labels
read grass fed
cage free
not tested on
funding alternatives

(the man
says fresh game
you huwoman beauty)

the board
said 100% ingredients
genuine produced
organic material
locally natural

the lawyer
read grass free
cage fed
not alternatives
funding tested on

(the woman
says the bones are not
so strange as the flesh)

Ballad of a Good Boy

in the park a sight yanks you back to 2013. see
the dog strain on the end of its lead. on the other side
two hands try to heel the barking from passing kids, poodles,
heedless couples. this animal is both stranger and self:
that man who dragged you to his office but also your own
desperation, those tugging eyes. it happened twice. the last
a woman from class padded up the stairwell. just as she
opened her mouth he dropped your bag, slammed his door.
   remember
learning to whine *it's okay it's fine* in the gum-bared tone
of every human who wants to believe *he's just playing*

Even Birds

For Faith

We arrive in Cambridge
after a long night's flight:
eighteen twenty-somethings
with a hangover of Africa.

What really matters, the man says,
is everyone's comfort.
We wouldn't want anyone
to be out
of place.
Don't ask and don't confess
potential transgressions.
This is a tour, after all.

So I keep clear of the line,
sick, tight with my truth.

Faith is still too
but later that night
she knocks on my door
and cries for skin
she's never been in.
These queer
constructs: towers cut
on ancestors' backs.

We discuss spectrums
of shame.

Late dawn is lilac
phosphorescence crossed
with migrating shadows.
There's no snow, just white ash.

Surely the others see;
they must sense our bent.
Even birds know silence
is also an answer.

Whale's Love Song

Some days it's unclear where the anchor is
but it holds in those submarine echoes,
the cetacean memories. The lean girl
said being lovesick is like falling in
the ocean: waves hit, but they're not heavy.
If only. Wipe out that tidal foam's light

droning. Infatuation is really
pulling seasick, so scared you'll make a mess,
so struck by each touch that you purge aright
to keep the foreseeable green at bay.
(Not that I can't trust, but just measure a
captain's log for sinking ships, whales that passed.)

And yet, with age comes the compulsion to
open fresh coves. Cut point breaks. Dissipate.
Feast on chances to witness weight, feel berthed;
honour bodies for moving, for strength's worth.

Bees never flew to me

Till I shaved an undercut
And tufts of fuzz
Drew the drones in

Till I learnt to wear neutral scents
Yuzu, lemongrass, basil leaves
Nectar for the swarm's dreams

Till I let my snarls curl
As both mankind and girl
Trapping honeybees like amber

The summer I cut old bows
Bees clung to my new clothes
First I was stung with fright
By their probing eyes

Then I realised their wisdom
Their buzzing redefining
What a queen means
So I froze and let them roam

Saying come for me
Sweethearts
I am no longer scared
Of what this body's meant to be

Hum

The hive is a giant
nose. See how communes sense
the queen's elation:
that mystic history of honey.
Today I hum, yellow,
rehearing your laughter
waxing in carnation.
Because you know me
down to my peeled feet.
Because your lashes furl
in subtlety. I know
no utopia is
what it seems, but oh,
this sweetness smells clean.

The Little Things

the way your puns still fall from north
to south like spokes wheeling
the hub of your mouth

when olive juice tends your hands
zest flecks my fingers
together we are kneading

how you noun the Latin in oilseed *rape*
find my favourite flavours grinning *eat*
both verbs now tame

what the bent hawthorn said
as you remembered us through rain
to the ancient oratory *he is good he is safe*

splitting sides or chores or dishes
the species you teach me naked swimming in oceans rivers baths
running tears I gasp to laugh at

the bearings found the screws that break
all growth a living poem
the fun home we make

Swimming Lessons

The boy from Bath asks
how warm home can be.
My nostrils freeze: the sting
of remembered chlorine.

And suddenly I'm five again
and stepping between
Jacaranda blooms,
alert for wiggling bees.

And I'm starting to swim
against the chlorine.

And suddenly it's adequate
and my limbs are elastic.
And I'm tasting the smell
of crushed marjoram.

And I'm holding my nose over
diaphanous chlorine.

And there are imitation cave paintings
chalked against moss.
And I'm tonguing a lemon
against grandmother's advice.

And I'm trying to breathe
against the chlorine.

Whatever the question was
he does not repeat.
Mark my accent, I'm still
learning to breathe.

ACKNOWLEDGEMENTS AND NOTES

Many thanks to the editors of the following journals for publishing some of these poems: *Aerodrome, Banshee, Epizootics, Gutter, Kalahari Review, New Coin, New Contrast, Ons Klyntji, Plumwood Mountain, PN Review, Poetry & Audience, SPAM, Stand, The Stockholm Review of Literature, Streetcake Magazine, Tears in the Fence, Tentacular, Type/Cast, uHlanga, Zoomorphic.*

Earlier versions of this collection were shortlisted for the Melita Hume Poetry Prize (2017) and the RædLeaf International Poetry Award (2016). Thank you to the judges for their supportive comments.

'Waking a Sleeping Rabbit by Surrounding Him with Grapes' was written in response to a video of the same name by YouTuber OneMorePlease. Thanks to Mike for granting permission to sample this video in a piece commissioned by Ilkley Literature Festival in 2021. Rest in peace, Pipkin.

The phrase 'deathsmilk' in 'A Fig' is taken from J.M. Coetzee's English translation of *Die kremetartekspedisie* by Wilma Stockenström.

'Echo's Reflection' was written for Rachelle Chadwick and Jabulile Mavuso, for inclusion in *Agenda* 35.4 (2021): a special issue on reproductive violence. This poem references a scene from Zoë Wicomb's *You Can't Get Lost in Cape Town*.

The first two lines of 'The Bridge' adapt lyrics from 'Bridge Song' by Julian Redpath.

Thanks to Benjamin Klein and Joe Shaughnessy for featuring 'Striking Rocks' in the Olive Schreiner Centenary Workshop at the University of Cambridge in 2020.

An earlier version of 'The Hit' appeared in *Poetry & Audience* 48.2. Thanks to the editorial team, particularly Emma Trott.

An earlier version of 'Offerings to a God' appeared in *Type/Cast* 1 as 'Offerings to the Gods'. Thanks to the editorial collective and especially guest editor Imraan Coovadia.

Thank you to the team at Osmosis Press for featuring an extract from 'Jealousy Experiment' on their website in 2021.

'W' is a response to Tony Harrison's 'V'.

'Gentled' is a response to Douglas Livingstone's 'Gentling a Wildcat'.

'Even Birds' was long listed for the 2016 Sol Plaatje EU Poetry Award and is published in an accompanying anthology.

'Whale's Love Song' was written for issue 17.3 of *Stand* on Ecopoetics (2019). Thanks to the editorial team and Anthony Vahni Capildeo for their continued encouragement.

The cover art of this book is a photograph by Zexi Xu, who kindly shared her research with me during the Leeds Creative Labs: Bragg Centre Edition. Thank you to Dagmara Kobza-Mroczkowska and Rashmi Seneviratne for also agreeing to share their research images in this collection. Thanks to Paul Beales and the broader Beales Research Group; 'Bilayer' and 'Frozen in time and space' were written as part of our collaboration *Blurred Lines: Life, Matter, Poetry*.

Many thanks to Stuart Bartholomew, Kobus Moolman, Louise Buchler, David Caddy, John Whale, Hannah Copley, Karen Tobias-Green, Lorna Dougan, Scott Mclaughlin, Stephen Manthorp, the Leeds Cultural Institute, Centre for Practice-Led Research in the Arts, University of Leeds Poetry Centre and Arts Council England for their generosity, guidance and support.

Thank you to Ryan Turnbull, Faith Pienaar, Peter Adkins, Diana De Ritter, Vic Clarke, Amber Lascelles, Adrienne Mortimer, Becky Macklin and Clare Fisher for years of friendship and motivation.

Thanks of course to my family for believing in my writing.

An ocean of thanks to Arththi Sathananthar, Kharys Ateh Laue and Saskia McCracken for attentive readings and careful comments on these poems.

ABOUT VERVE POETRY PRESS

Verve Poetry Press is a quite new and already award-winning press that focused initially on meeting a local need in Birmingham - a need for the vibrant poetry scene here in Brum to find a way to present itself to the poetry world via publication. Co-founded by Stuart Bartholomew and Amerah Saleh, it now publishes poets from all corners of the UK - poets that speak to the city's varied and energetic qualities and will contribute to its many poetic stories.

Added to this is a colourful pamphlet series, many featuring poets who have performed at our sister festival - and a poetry show series which captures the magic of longer poetry performance pieces by festival alumni such as Polarbear, Matt Abbott and Genevieve Carver.

The press has been voted Most Innovative Publisher at the Saboteur Awards, and has won the Publisher's Award for Poetry Pamphlets at the Michael Marks Awards.

Like the festival, we strive to think about poetry in inclusive ways and embrace the multiplicity of approaches towards this glorious art.

www.vervepoetrypress.com
@VervePoetryPres
mail@vervepoetrypress.com